C000061215

FILLIN' UP

REAL ESTATE RESCUE COZY MYSTERIES, BOOK 11

PATTI BENNING

SUMMER PRESCOTT BOOKS PUBLISHING

CHAPTER ONE

Flora Abner stood in the entryway of her house. Beautiful, shining hardwood floors extended down the hall that led past the stairs to the kitchen. The trim was pristine white, not a scuff or a smudge on it. The walls were a soft, pale blue-gray, and the air smelled like buttery cookies, thanks to her newest candle.

After a little more than a year and a half of hard work, the once-neglected house was just about perfect. The roof no longer leaked. All the water damage had been patched over, the once dry and scratched floors had been refinished, and the kitchen counters had been redone. The house was over a hundred years old, and while she had kept the old farmhouse charm, it didn't feel its age any longer. It felt comfortable, cozy, and sturdy enough to stand another hundred years. It felt like a home.

Flora took a deep breath and lowered her phone. She had been comparing the entranceway to one of the photos she had taken when she first moved here. Even though she had done the vast majority of the work herself, the comparison still astounded her. She felt a bittersweet mixture of pride and wistfulness as she considered the progress she had made.

She was making huge strides toward her desired career as a house flipper, but she had made one big mistake. She had fallen in love with this house. Selling it was going to be difficult.

That didn't mean she wasn't going to put her best effort into it, of course. With all of the big repairs out of the way, it was time to focus on the little things. Right now, most of her furniture was the cheapest secondhand stuff she had been able to find. It was fine for her, but in just a few months, she was going to start the process of getting the house listed. She had done a lot of research about selling houses, and she knew just how much difference a good set of photos could make. She had to pay her aunt back a sizable loan, and she also needed to make enough money to get started on fixing up the next house she bought, which meant she had to sell this house for top dollar.

Anyone who looked at the listing had to fall love with the place. And that meant doing something about her ragtag collection of furniture.

She wasn't going to get rid of what she already had, but she could store it in the nice, rebuilt shed behind the house while she found some nicer pieces to showcase in the listing pictures. She could also offer to let the furniture go with the house, which might help the sale.

It was time to say a temporary goodbye to her ratty old pullout couch, the comfortable yet worn recliner, and the coffee table someone's puppy had chewed on a lifetime ago.

"We're in the homestretch now, Amaretto," she told her fluffy white Persian cat as she walked into the living room.

Amaretto was in her customary spot on the back of the couch, gazing out the window to the porch and the dirt road and field beyond. Although Flora vacuumed the couch whenever she cleaned the floors, there always seemed to be a layer of white fur where Amaretto liked to lay. She was already planning to send the cat to stay in her friend's apartment when she started showing the house, both to keep Amaretto out of way of the viewers, and to make sure the cat didn't slip out during a showing and get lost in the woods...

and also to keep the amount of fur in the house down to a negligible level.

That was still a few months away, though, so for now she contented herself with running her fingers through the cat's long, silky coat, and casting a judgmental eye around the living room.

It would be nice to get a matching set of furniture, but she wasn't going to fork over the money to purchase something brand-new. She hadn't used up all of the loan her aunt had given her, and she didn't want to. She was going to have to pay it all back before long. Her own, personal income from the hardware store was enough for the essentials, but she wasn't going to get rich off of it anytime soon. Her business partner and boyfriend, Grady, took home the bigger salary since he was the majority owner of the business and also put in the most hours there. She split her time between the hardware store and her home, and she knew once she moved on to her next flipping project, she would have even less time to put in at the store. In other words, money was tight, even if things weren't desperate yet.

"I'm sure whatever house we buy next will have a view you enjoy just as much," she told the cat. "No more apartments for us."

It was nice having more space. She had found that

she enjoyed hosting get-togethers for her friends. Sydney's birthday was next week, and they were going to have the party here, with no worries about disturbing her neighbors.

The cat's tail twitched in response to her words, or maybe in response to the bird that had landed on the porch railing. Even though neither of them moved, the bird took off in a sudden, alarmed flutter of feathers. Flora shifted to look out the window from a better angle and spotted her elderly neighbor, Beth York, coming up the driveway with her droopy Basset hound beside her.

At the sight of the dog, Amaretto's tail puffed up and she darted off the couch. Flora sighed. She loved dogs, but she didn't think owning one would be in the cards for her, not while she had Amaretto. The cat couldn't stand them.

She walked over to the front door and pulled it open, slipping out while blocking the exit with her legs out of habit, since Amaretto had a bad tendency to try to dart outside whenever the door opened. Shutting the door behind her, she waved to her neighbor, who waved cheerily back.

"What a nice morning," Beth called out. "Are you doing well, dear?"

Barefoot, Flora lingered on the porch as Beth

approached. Sammy, the Basset hound, paused to sniff intently at a patch of grass in her yard. Beth lingered while he examined it.

"I'm feeling a little sentimental today, I think," she said. "It *is* a nice day, though. How was your morning walk?"

"It was lovely," Beth said. "This autumn weather is my favorite, and I think Sammy likes it too. The summers are just too hot for us. Enjoy your youth while you have it, Flora. Once you reach my age, you'll constantly be either too hot or too cold. Sometimes both at once, if you're unlucky."

"This is my favorite sort of weather too," Flora said. "I've always loved fall. Do you want to come in, or are you just stopping by for a chat?"

"I just thought I'd swing by and say hello," Beth said. "You should join us on our walks sometimes, dear. I've seen you out with that cat of yours on her leash. Maybe she would get more used to Sammy if they took some walks together."

She thought there was a much greater chance that Amaretto would squirm out of her harness and hide at the top of a tree, but she didn't say that. Still, Beth had become a good friend to her over the past year and a half. She could always go on a walk without her cat.

"Maybe next time. If I spot you going by tomorrow, I'll pop out and join you."

"That would be wonderful," Beth said. "What do you have on your plate today?"

"Furniture shopping," Flora told her. "Or at least, browsing. I want to get some nice, matching furniture for the house. I don't want to buy it new, though, and the thrift store usually has a random assortment of pieces. Do you know any secondhand furniture stores that might have matching sets?"

"I'm afraid not," Beth said, her brow furrowing as she thought. After a moment, her expression brightened. "A friend of mine is having an estate sale this weekend. I think it starts tomorrow. She has some lovely furniture, and I think she's selling almost everything. Her husband passed away last month, and she's moving into assisted living."

"Oh, that's horrible," Flora said.

"I don't think it was unexpected," Beth said. "If you get me a notepad, I'll write down her information for you. I think you'll be able to find some lovely items there."

"I'd appreciate that," Flora said. "Let me just go grab a pen and some paper. I'll be right back."

She popped back inside to fetch the supplies. With anyone else, she would have had them type the information out on her phone, but Beth wasn't a fan of touch screens, or technology in general. Flora had been helping her with the ancient desktop she and her husband owned, and while Beth was now able to get news from the town's social media page and check local business hours online, Flora was certain she didn't enjoy the experience.

Using the porch railing to support the notepad, Beth wrote down the name *Marjorie Beckman*, and then an address underneath it before handing the notepad back to Flora.

"If you end up buying anything from her, I'd love to see whatever you get," Beth told her. "I'd best be getting back home with Sammy now. Tim will be wanting his breakfast soon. You have a nice day, dear."

"You have a nice day too, Beth. I'll see you later."

She watched as the elderly woman and her dog tottered off down the street, then slipped back inside to figure out how far away the address was and see if Grady wanted to go with her tomorrow.

She hoped she had similar tastes to Beth's friend. It would be nice to knock all of the furniture shopping out in one trip.

CHAPTER TWO

Flora pulled up to the curb in front of the apartment building across from the hardware store at nine the next morning. She and Grady had gotten involved in some deadly drama surrounding an apartment for rent a couple of months ago, and once the apartment was unexpectedly available again, he had realized that not only could he now afford to live there, but that living right across from the hardware store made a lot of sense.

Leaving the trailer he used to call home to his brother, Wade, he made the move, and was now settled into the little two-bedroom apartment where he could look out the window and see the hardware store across the street.

Since their only employee, Ellison, was now

experienced enough to open and close the store on his own, Grady had more time off than he was used to. This was one of the mornings neither of them was working, and he had been happy to accept her invitation to go furniture shopping at the estate sale today. Since the house was in town, not far from his apartment, she had offered to pick him up on her way.

Now, she got out of her truck and made her way toward the door that led up to the apartment. Before she could press the buzzer, it opened and Grady came out.

"Hey, I saw you pull up," he said, pulling her in for a hug. "Did you have a good morning?"

"I spent most of it drinking coffee and watching Amaretto get increasingly frustrated at a brave little bird that kept hopping around on the windowsill," she said. "You?"

"Still getting used to living in this place," he said. "It's kind of nice to be in town, though. I saw Ellison arrive at the hardware store a couple hours ago. It's hard to see the hardware store and not feel like I should be there."

"You're allowed to have a life outside of work," she said, nudging him with her elbow as they walked toward her truck. "Life's pretty good, isn't it?"

"Yeah, sometimes I still can't believe how well things have gone these past couple of years."

Life had its ups and downs, but for both of them, there had been more ups than downs. To Flora, who came from a well-off family in Chicago, it was business as usual. For Grady, who had spent his life in a trailer park in the poorer part of the small, rural town of Warbler, Kentucky, the larger salary he had as a business owner instead of an employee at the hardware store and finally moving into a nice apartment had been a big change for him.

He paused before they reached her truck. "Actually, now that I think about it, if you're looking for furniture, it might make more sense if we drive separately. We'll be able to haul more large items if we have both trucks with us."

"You're right," she said. "I didn't even think of that. I don't know how much I'll buy, or if I'll even buy anything, but if I do end up buying a whole set of furniture, I'd rather not to have to come back for a second trip."

"I'll walk over to the hardware store and grab my truck," he told her. "Then I'll follow you over to the house the sale is at."

She nodded and got into her own truck to wait for him. Even though the apartment building offered on-street parking, he preferred to park his truck in the hardware store's parking lot. She didn't blame him – something about parking on the street felt a lot less secure.

When she saw him pull the truck out of the hardware store's lot, she put on her blinker and pulled away from the curb. Her GPS was already set to Marjorie Beckman's house, which was only a few blocks away. Almost everything in Warbler was only a few blocks away from the hardware store, which was one of the upsides of living in such a small town.

Even without looking at the address, it was obvious which house had the estate sale going on when she turned onto the street. The driveway was packed with cars, and so was the curb in front of it. Flora found a spot to park, and watched Grady drive partway down the block to claim his own space. She waited for him on the sidewalk, and they walked up to the house together.

It was a towering old Victorian home, with an iron fence in the back and a tall, peaked roof with twin turrets rising on either side of the house. The yard was impeccably cared for, and even the grass had an expensive feel as they walked across it.

Her house and yard were nice. This was on a different level entirely.

"I hope I can afford whatever she's selling," Flora murmured. "I was hoping to *save* money by getting secondhand furniture, not spend a fortune."

"It'll still be fun to look, even if you don't end up getting anything," he said. She nodded – it would be a lot of fun to look through everything that was for sale in this house. Even if she didn't get any furniture, she might be able to find a few pieces of decor she liked.

There was a table set up in front of the house that seemed to be working as a sign-in booth. She and Grady joined the short line, but it soon became obvious it wasn't moving. A glance to the front of it told her why.

An elderly woman with a shock of white hair that was puffed around her head like a cloud was standing over the middle-aged woman who was seated at the table, her hands planted on her hips.

"The floors getting filthy," the elderly woman snapped, in what sounded like the latest of a long line of complaints. "I've asked you three times already to tell everyone to wipe their feet coming in, and to avoid walking on the grass when they leave. And *no children*. Someone brought their five-year-old in, and she almost knocked over a vase. I was told your company was professional, but if it is, I have yet to see it. This is the furthest thing from the stress-free experience you promised me. You won't be getting a tip from *me,* I guarantee it."

"Please, Ms. Beckman," the woman said, sounding weary. "I assure you, I'm doing the best I can. You should be glad it's so busy today. You'll be sure to sell almost everything by the end of the weekend."

"I should never have agreed to this," Marjorie Beckman muttered as she turned away to stalk back inside. "Strangers tramping through my home all weekend… this is a nightmare."

The woman at the table let her shoulders droop in relief and started moving the line along again. She looked a little more relaxed by the time Flora and Grady reached her.

"Welcome to the Beckman Estate Sale," she said. "My name is Sherry Roper, and I'm here to help with whatever you need. Please sign in with at least one of your names and your phone number, along with the time you arrived. If you see an item you want, please remove its tag and come here to this table to pay. If you pay cash, you can take it home with you today. If you wish to pay with a check or a card, you will have to wait until Monday to pick up your items, so I can ensure the payment clears. Any questions?"

"I don't think so," Flora said as she wrote down

her name and her phone number on the list. The paper's heading read *Lorelei's Estate Solutions*. She asked Grady to check the time before she wrote that down as well. "Actually, I do have one. Is the sale throughout the whole house, or are there areas that are off limits?"

She didn't want to do something to draw Marjorie Beckman's ire. The woman seemed to be in a terrible mood today. Flora couldn't quite blame her, considering the circumstances. Losing both her husband and her independence all in the span of a couple of months would put anyone in a bad mood.

Sherry shook her head. "You're free to wander. If a door's locked, don't try to open it, but I think the only room that's off limits is the owner's bedroom. I hope you find some lovely items to purchase today."

As Sherry turned to the next person, Flora and Grady entered the house. It was just as elegant inside as it was on the outside. Flora hoped that one day she could get her hands on a house like this. The dramatic, curved staircase, the beautiful dark wood floors and high ceilings… she was in love.

"What sort of furniture you looking for?" Grady asked from beside her. He was peering at a dark mahogany end table with lions' paws carved at the ends of the legs.

"I'm not sure," she admitted. "I don't want something so fancy it's going to overshadow the house. It should look nice, but not… pretentious, you know?"

He raised an eyebrow and looked around. "I'm not sure you'll find that here."

Flora was beginning to have her doubts as well. Everything in the house was *nice*, but it looked expensive, and none of it seemed like it would fit her cozy little farmhouse very well. Still, she wanted to walk around for a while. There was a lot of neat stuff in here, and there was no harm in looking.

They moved through the house slowly, occasionally having to move aside to let someone else through. They were examining a painting on the wall at the bottom of the staircase that showed a Greek woman reclining in a field of flowers when a middle-aged man with curly, light brown pushed past Grady forcefully before hurrying up the stairs, a single piece of paper clutched in one hand.

Grady stumbled into Flora, they both turned to look at the man as he rushed upstairs.

"That was rude," Grady muttered.

Flora frowned in agreement. "He could've at least said excuse me."

They turned back to the painting, but Flora knew there was no way she was going to buy it, not for the nearly five-thousand-dollar price tag. Just before they turned away, they heard an argument break out upstairs, and turned to look up the stairwell again.

They couldn't make out the words, but it sounded like two women were really getting into it. A door slammed, and a moment later, an elderly woman appeared at the top of the stairs. She wasn't Marjorie, though – this woman had dark gray hair pulled back into a tight bun, and held the railing carefully as she descended. Despite her caution on the stairs, her face and body language were practically screaming with rage, and Flora and Grady stepped neatly out of the way before she got to the bottom of the steps. She stalked past them without a glance in their direction. They exchanged a look, and glanced up the stairs.

This whole visit was already a lot more exciting than Flora had expected.

She moved to the side as someone else went up the stairs, taking a step back onto a nice runner rug that went down the hallway. She paused, considering it. It would actually look very nice in *her* hallway. It had soft creams and blues, and she thought it would go wonderfully with her walls. She looked around, but didn't see a tag on it.

"Do you think this rug is for sale?" she asked Grady.

He looked down at it, one eyebrow rising. "I've got no idea. We could go ask that woman. What was her name?"

"Sherry," Flora said. They moved toward the front door and looked outside, but the table was empty. People were signing themselves in, and Sherry was nowhere to be seen.

"Let's see if we can find her," she said.

They wandered the first floor of the house, but they couldn't find Sherry anywhere. Finally, they decided to head up the stairs. Flora lingered on the curving staircase, running her hand along the banister. She was getting so many ideas from this house, she could hardly wait to put them into use with the next house she flipped.

There was a hallway at the top of the stairs that went to the left and right. It seemed quieter up here, with only one person standing in the hall to the right, examining some artwork. They decided to go left, and walked down the hall together, peeking into rooms as they went by. The door at the end of the hall was partially open, but the light inside the room was off, while the lights in all the other rooms had been on. Flora hesitated, but Sherry had said the only room they weren't allowed in would be locked. She pushed the door open and felt around on the wall for a light switch. It was one of the ones she had to twist. The light came on, dim at first, then brighter. She tried to push the door further open, but it bumped into something and wouldn't budge.

Wondering if someone had knocked something over, she squeezed through the gap between the door and the doorframe and entered the room. As soon as she saw what was blocking the door, she froze.

Marjorie Beckman was laying on her back on the floor, her white hair spread out around her head like a halo. A wound on her temple had stained some of it red, and her eyes stared blankly up at Flora.

She was dead.

CHAPTER THREE

Grady must have been concerned at her reaction, because he poked his head into the room to see what she was looking at. When he cursed, low and under his breath, it snapped her out of her shock enough to get her moving again. She squeezed through the door and back into the hall, then pulled it firmly shut behind her.

"It would be nice if Sherry hadn't up and vanished," she muttered. Her heart was pounding, and she was glad the second floor wasn't as crowded as the first. As soon as people learned Marjorie had passed away, there was sure to be panic.

"I'll make the call," Grady volunteered after peering at her face for a moment. She felt a rush of gratitude toward him. She was on much more familiar terms with everyone at the police station than he was, and was usually the one to call in when they needed the authorities, but right now, she could barely focus. Her mind kept replaying the moment she found the body over and over again.

While he took out his cell phone and dialed the number, she kept her back pressed firmly to the door, hoping no one else came along and wanted to get into the room. She was only half aware of the sound of Grady talking to the dispatcher, too lost in her thoughts to catch his words.

What had happened to the elderly woman? Was it an accident... or murder? The argument they had heard the tail end of not long before made her wonder, but she didn't want to jump to conclusions. Perhaps Marjorie had simply tripped and fell -- a tragedy, but not a crime.

The sound of a toilet flushing from a room down the hall drew her eyes in that direction. The man who had been looking at paintings was gone, and she had thought they were alone up here, but evidentially not.

A door past the stairway opened, and Sherry stepped out. Flora stared at her for a moment. If they had gone the other direction when they first came up here, they would have found her, asked about the rug, and been on their way. Not for the first time, she wondered if there was something to Officer Hendrick's jokes about her bad luck.

Sherry spotted them, but seemed distracted. Her gaze wandered past them as she patted her hands on her shirt. There was a wet spot on the front, near the collar, as if she had rinsed a stain off it in the restroom. Suddenly, her eyes snapped back to Flora.

"Oh, that's the bedroom, miss," she said, moving toward them. "It should be locked -- that room isn't open to the public."

Flora glanced at Grady out of the corner of her eye, but he was busy giving directions to the house on his phone -- he likely hadn't remembered the address, so had to describe how to find it in detail. This was up to her. It was a good thing Sherry was the first person they had seen, at least. She would hopefully be able to close down the sale and keep panic to a minimum.

Not wanting to interrupt Grady's conversation with the dispatcher, she met the other woman partway down the hall. She didn't know what her expression looked like, but it must have been bad, because Sherry's lips twitched down in a frown.

"There's been an accident," she said, keeping her voice low. "We found Marjorie in her bedroom."

"I'm afraid I don't understand."

"It... it looks like she fell," Flora said. There was

no point in mentioning the argument right now. It would just confuse things. "She's passed away."

Maybe she shouldn't be dancing around the subject, but she couldn't force herself to come out and say "she's dead." Getting these softer words out was hard enough.

Sherry gave her an uncomprehending look until slowly, a look of horrified realization dawned on her face. "What? Show me?"

Flora hesitated, not sure if that was a good idea or not, but Sherry didn't wait for her. She pushed past Flora in the narrow hall, stepped past Grady, who gave Flora a wide-eyed look that she returned with a helpless one of her own, and turned the doorknob to the bedroom.

She leaned in through the door, then quickly backed out, shutting it quietly behind her. Her eyes were wide, and she took a deep, shaky breath.

"I need to get everyone out of the house," she said, seemingly half to herself. "This estate sale needs to end right now. No more sales. And the police -- oh, goodness, this is too much."

"Grady's already talking to the police," Flora said, hoping to help the woman calm down a little. She was beginning to look a little pale. "What do you need? I can help."

Sherry gave her a wide-eyed stare for a moment before becoming all business. "I need you to go turn people away at the door. *Don't* tell them why. I'm going to go through the house and ask everyone who's currently here to leave."

Grady covered the microphone on his cell phone with his hand as he said, "I'll keep watch on the bedroom, and I won't let anyone in."

Sherry nodded briskly, and the two of them hopped to it. Flora hurried downstairs, ignoring the other shoppers at the estate sale, since Sherry had said she would handle them. She slipped out the front door and approached the table with the sign-in sheet. It might be evidence, if the police ruled Marjorie's death as a homicide, so she subtly slid it closer to her before she addressed the people who had been about to sign in.

"I'm sorry, but the estate sale is closing early today. No one else can go in. If you're with someone who already went inside, you're welcome to wait out here. They will be sent out shortly."

"What happened?" a woman a few years older than Flora asked. "I drove all the way here from McKee."

"There's been, um, a medical emergency," Flora said. It was sort of the truth, and wouldn't worry people as much as what had really happened. The last thing they needed was a huge crowd of curious people to overwhelm the police when they arrived.

Thankfully, no one argued too much. The people who had been waiting in line turned away and began to leave, some of them muttering to each other. She glanced down at the sign-in sheet, wondering if Marjorie's death had truly been an accident, or if the name of her killer was somewhere on there.

A squeal of tires tore her attention away from the paper, and she looked up to see a minivan pull away from the curb fast enough that one of the people who was walking back to their car had to jump back to avoid being struck. She watched it go, her surprise at the noise quickly turning to suspicion. Were they fleeing the scene? Unfortunately, her realization had come too slow -- the minivan was already turning the corner, and she couldn't get a good look at the license plate.

One by one, people streamed out through the front door, walking past the table with concerned or upset expressions on their faces. She watched them go, wondering what Sherry had told them. She had to stay at her spot on the table, since even as people left, others pulled up along the curb and got out of their cars, hoping to see the estate sale. Thankfully, the police didn't take long to arrive, and with their vehicles parked in the driveway, the stream of hopeful shoppers stopped coming.

When Grady came out of the house, she quickly took a photo of the sign-in sheet, then walked over to join him in telling the police what had happened. By now, the initial shock was beginning to fade, and she felt jittery and a little sick, as if she had drunk too much coffee.

Had Marjorie met her natural end at the worst of all possible times, or had someone murdered her during the estate sale?

This was not how she expected the day to go. She hadn't even gotten a chance to ask about that rug.

CHAPTER FOUR

After a somber drive back to Grady's apartment and an equally somber talk, the *last* thing Flora wanted to do was stop at Beth's house and give her the bad news, but there was no getting out of it. Beth deserved to know what had happened to her friend, and she deserved to hear it firsthand.

It was barely past noon when she pulled her truck into Beth's driveway, but it felt like it should be later. It should be a dark and stormy evening, not a cheery afternoon.

She took a moment to just sit in her truck's cab and gather her thoughts. When she was ready, she shut the engine off and got out. It was a warm day, for all that it was autumn, and for a moment she imagined what a different version of herself would be doing, one that hadn't found a body while shopping for furniture. Would she be unrolling the runner rug in her hallway, and offering Grady a lemonade before they went outside to sit on her porch?

That version of herself would never come to be. Taking a deep, bracing breath, she walked up to Beth's front door and knocked on it, then waited. It often took Beth some time to get to her feet, but after a minute, the door opened and her friend looked out.

"What a pleasant surprise! Good afternoon, dear. What can I do for you?"

Flora took a deep breath. "Can I come in? I've got some sad news."

The two of them sat at Beth's kitchen table while Flora told her everything that had happened at the estate sale. She witnessed the older woman go through the stages of grief, seemingly all in the span of the ten minutes the tale took.

Perhaps at her age, Beth was used to losing people, or maybe she simply hadn't liked Marjorie that much. Flora wasn't sure which it was, especially considering what Beth said in response to the news.

"How horrible. Poor Marjorie. It sounds like someone might have done her in. I can't say I'm terribly surprised it happened, of course."

"Why is that?" Flora asked. She had been

expecting more tears and less... this. She couldn't imagine hearing that one of her friends had died -- possibly been murdered -- and calmly saying, *Ah, that makes sense.*

"Marjorie, may she rest in peace, made enemies like I make tea. I couldn't tell you how many people she's driven to tears or mad with anger over the years. Did I tell you how she met her most recent husband?"

"Most *recent* husband?"

"He was her third -- she's been divorced twice. I do believe she loved him, and I know she was utterly stricken when he passed, but he was perhaps the only person who reliably got any shred of kindness from her. He was married when they met, but it didn't stay that way for long. He left his wife for her, and she made no pretense about what she was doing. Of course, that was two decades ago now, but you should have heard the rumor mill in town at the time! It was all any of us could talk about."

"So her husband's ex-wife would definitely have a grudge against her?" she asked, thinking of the woman who had come down the stairs after the argument she and Grady had overheard.

"I'm certain of it, but she moved away shortly after the divorce. Couldn't stand everyone in town knowing what had happened. No, what I was getting at was her stepson. Benny Beckman. He still lives in town, poor thing, but the divorce cost him *both* his parents. I heard Marjorie wouldn't so much as let her husband speak with him after they married, and I heard whispers that he knew about the affair while it was happening, and so his mother cut ties with him as well, for keeping it a secret. I spoke to Marjorie about it once, asking if maybe she shouldn't try to include the man in holidays, at the very least, but she nearly laughed in my face. She didn't want any reminders of her husband's previous life, I think."

"No offense, Beth, but she sounds pretty unpleasant. Why were you friends with her, exactly?"

"We both grew up here," Beth said. "I don't think you'd understand, dear. You're too young, and you haven't been here all your life. She wasn't my friend in the same way you're friends with that lovely Violet girl. She was a friend of familiarity and shared history. We spent nearly eighty years in the same town, attending the same events, knowing the same people. I didn't like her all the time, but we certainly had a lot of shared experiences to speak about." She sighed. "When you get to be my age, you'll understand. At some point, your friends start dropping like flies, and you look around and realize that suddenly your worst enemy is one of the only people in the world you can reminisce with, and it changes things."

They were silent for a moment, the heavy conversation more suffocating than most of what they usually talked about. Finally, Flora asked, "What about that woman I described? The one with the bun? Do you have any idea who she might be?"

"Did she have a very strict expression, like a school marm?"

"Yes? I guess that's how you could describe it."

Beth nodded briskly. "Then I'm nearly certain that was Eloise Brown. She and Marjorie go way back, and I was never quite able to tell if they were the closest of friends or the worst of enemies. Sometimes they would have fights and wouldn't speak for months, and then all of a sudden, I would see them getting lunch together as if nothing had happened. If someone picked an argument with Marjorie during the estate sale, I'd put my money on it being Eloise."

"Do you think she might have had something to do with Marjorie's death?"

"I can't imagine she would do something so horrible on purpose," Beth said. "And what would the point be? Marjorie was selling everything, and then moving. If Eloise finally snapped and wanted her gone, all she would have had to do was wait a few weeks, and Marjorie would be tucked away at an assisted living community in the city, no murder necessary."

"Maybe it wasn't planned," Flora mused. "It could have been a spur of the moment thing, or even an accident. An argument that got out of hand."

"It's possible," Beth said. "If I see her when I'm in town this weekend, I'll see what she has to say." She leaned forward to pat Flora's hand across the table. "Thank you for coming to talk with me, dear. I'm ever so glad you moved here. You're a very kind girl."

Flora was touched, but in the back of her mind, she wondered if she had ever told Beth she was planning on selling the house and moving come spring. She was certain she had mentioned she was going to flip the house back when she first moved here... hadn't she?

A dull dread settled into her stomach as she said goodbye to Beth and drove the short distance home. If Beth didn't know Flora's stay was only ever meant to be temporary, then she wasn't sure how she would break it to the older woman. They had grown close over almost two years of knowing each other, and while Flora planned to stay in the area for at least another two years and would visit Beth, it just wouldn't be the same as living right down the road from her.

Another thought struck her; if whoever bought the house next year was a bad neighbor, Beth was never going to let her hear the end of it.

CHAPTER FIVE

As much as Marjorie's death had impacted Flora, there was surprisingly little news about what had happened over the next few days. Not one person said anything about it during Flora's shifts at the hardware store that weekend, and even Violet and Sydney only knew about it because Flora and Grady told them.

Maybe she shouldn't have been surprised. After all, an elderly woman passing away in her own home was hardly newsworthy. As far as Flora knew, there was no clear sign that her death had been a homicide. A bump on the head could happen to anyone. She was sure the coroner would do an investigation, but until that came through and the police were notified of any red flags -- if there even were any -- then her death was unremarkable, as cold as the thought was.

She felt a little guilty for things getting back to normal as quickly as they did. By Tuesday, she had mostly put the incident out of her mind. She still had her suspicions, but there wasn't anything she could do about it. She had no evidence, nothing except a single argument she hadn't even been able to properly over-hear and the knowledge that Marjorie was better at making enemies than friends. The only thing she could do was move on.

Which was why she was so surprised when the unknown number that called her on her cell phone during the last hour of the morning shift at the hard-ware store turned out to be Sherry Roper, the woman who had been running the estate sale.

"Is this Flora Abner?" Sherry sounded stressed, and for the first time, Flora wondered how this was affecting her. She had to be taking it even harder than Flora was -- she may not have *found* the body, but she had seen it, and she had been the one in charge of the whole event.

"Yes, it's me," Flora said. She made an apologetic face to Ellison before she stepped into an empty aisle to continue the conversation in private.

"Thank goodness. I couldn't tell if the last digit was a three or an eight. Can you remind me if you bought anything at Marjorie Beckman's estate sale?"

"No, we didn't have time," Flora said, sparing a sad thought for the pretty rug she had missed out on.

"That's what I thought." Sherry sounded disappointed and exhausted.

"You're not facing any repercussions for what happened, are you?" Sherry might have been the one in charge, but Flora didn't think it was fair for her to take any blame for Marjorie's death. No one could have guessed how the day would end.

"Not for the death, no," Sherry said. "But when I took an inventory of the house after everyone left, I noticed some items were missing. Items I didn't remember selling... and some were quite pricey. Whoever ends up inheriting the estate is going to have some questions, and I'm trying to cover my bases."

"Do you think someone stole the missing items?"

"That's what I'm worried about," Sherry admitted. "The one I'm most concerned about is a painting, worth nearly five-thousand dollars. It was hanging at the bottom of the stairs. I didn't even know it was missing until I did the inventory. I'm certain I didn't sell *that*, but there are some smaller items missing as well -- some vases and figurines, and a set of nice silverware. Real silverware. I've been calling everyone who came in the last hour, just to make sure

I didn't somehow miss a sale when things were getting busy."

"Are you talking about the painting of a Greek or Roman woman in a field of flowers?"

"Yes, Do you remember it?"

"I do. Grady and I were looking at it just a few minutes before we found Marjorie."

"That means whoever took it has to have been there during the last ten minutes before I closed the sale down. Please, think back. You didn't see *anyone* who was acting suspicious?"

Flora frowned. "Well, I did see a minivan pull away when I went outside to tell people no one else could go in. They pulled away from the curb fast enough to make the tires squeal. It stood out to me, and I mentioned it to the police."

"That has to be it," Sherry said. "Did you get the license plate number? What did the van look like?"

"I wasn't fast enough to see the license plate, but the van was light blue. Have you reported the theft to the police?"

"Not yet, I was hoping it was just some sort of misunderstanding, but you're one of the last names on my list. I'm going to have to make a report unless a miracle happens and someone wrote me a five-thousand dollar check I somehow forgot about." She sighed. "Thanks for answering my call. I've got a little more to go on now, at least."

They said their goodbyes and Flora ended the call, slipping her cell phone back into her back pocket. She wondered if she should have said something about the woman with the bun in her hair, Eloise, but she had left before the painting went missing. She clearly remembered looking at the painting right before moving to the side so Eloise could get past.

She had no idea whether Eloise was responsible for Marjorie's death, but she didn't think she had anything to do with the missing items.

Lost in thought, she wandered back to the front desk. She had spent a good portion of her shift trying to straighten out a shipping error that had send them a thousand box cutters instead of a hundred, but the shipping company didn't accept returns, so they were probably going to be running a sale on box cutters for a *long* time to come. Ellison was currently working on designing a poster for the sale on the computer, and turned the screen to show her when she reached the counter.

"What do you think? Too cheerful?"

"I think it looks good," she told him. "It's certainly eye-catching."

"Do you think Grady will like it?"

"I don't think I'll ever say this again, and don't quote me on it, but in the particular instance I'm tempted to say Grady doesn't get a say. He's the one who typed an extra zero into the order form, and that was the worst call to a manufacturer I've had to deal with yet, so I'm taking away his veto power for this."

Ellison grinned and sent an order to the printer in the back room to print off five of the posters. She hoped they had enough ink left. They were very brightly colored.

"Is everything all right?" he asked once he closed the art program. "I wasn't going to ask, but you seem kind of upset after that call."

"It's nothing," she said. "Well, not nothing, but it's nothing I can do anything about. I just feel bad for the woman who called me. She was in charge of an estate sale, and some expensive items went missing. She's trying to track them down."

"She should check local sales listings online," he suggested. "My sister's laptop got stolen in her first week at college, and she found it posted for sale in a local buy and sell group a week later and managed to get the police involved and get it back. They said that sort of thing happens more than we'd think. I guess most thieves aren't the sharpest box cutter in the box."

He grinned at his own joke, and she gave a snort of laughter despite her mood. "Maybe I'll give her a call later and suggest it." She couldn't imagine the thief selling a five-thousand-dollar painting in the local buy and sell group, but maybe some of the smaller items would show up. "My shift's over soon. Did you need help with anything before I go?"

"Actually, yeah." He picked a small pile of papers up off the counter and handed them to her. "These are the applications you asked me to print out. I disabled the online form at noon, so we won't get any more unless someone drops one off in person."

"Thanks, Ellison," she said, taking the papers. "I'll look these over with Grady. You'll be working with whoever we hire, so if you've got any feedback about the people who applied in person, feel free to chime in."

"The two applications at the top belong to friends of mine," he admitted. "Either of them really would be a good fit, though."

"Oh. Well, in that case, shuffle these up for me while I go grab my purse and jacket out of the back, would you? I don't want to be biased while I'm looking over the applications for the first time."

He nodded and took the papers back from her while she slipped into the back room to pick up her jacket and purse, and paused to shoot a glare at the box of box cutters. It was going to take them *years* to sell all of those, and the customer service representative she had spoken to had not been helpful in the least.

A customer had come in while she was in the back; she almost ran into him when she pushed the storeroom door open. She uttered a reflexive apology, but he ignored her. When she glanced back, she saw the curly-haired man looking around with an expression that had become all too familiar with her over her time working here.

He had no idea what aisle whatever he was looking for was in.

Her shift wasn't over yet, and even if it was, she would have lingered to help out a customer, so she said, "Is there anything I can help you with, sir?"

He turned to face her with a wince. "Yes, do you sell lock boxes? I thought I saw them here before, but you must have reorganized, because I thought they were back here."

"They're over at the end of aisle eight," she told him. "Would you like me to take you to them?"

"No, I can probably find them myself. Thanks."

He walked off, and she made her way back toward the front of the store. Something about that man seemed familiar. Where had she seen him before? He couldn't be a regular if he hadn't been in since they reorganized.

Her steps faltered as she realized why he was so familiar. *He* was the rude man who had shoved past Grady in his hurry to get up the stairs at the estate sale. Come to think of it, where had he gone after climbing the stairs? He wasn't the same man who had been looking at the art in the upstairs hallway, and she hadn't seen him the entire time she and Grady were standing in front of Marjorie's door, trying to figure out what to do. It was like he had vanished once he reached the top of the stairs.

She had completely forgotten about him until now. Hurrying back to the front counter, she settled in to wait for the man to check out instead of leaving like she had planned. Ellison took the opportunity to go hang his box cutter sale posters up around the store while she waited.

Finally, the mysterious rude man approached the counter with a hefty lockbox in his cart. As she scanned it, she wondered why he was buying it. Was it a coincidence, or was it for something like hiding stolen valuables? It wouldn't fit the painting, of course, but could probably fit the silverware and quite a few figurines.

The man seemed to be in a hurry, and tapped his fingers impatiently on the counter as she rang him up and told him the total. "Will you be paying with cash or card?"

"Card."

She pressed the corresponding button and watched as he slid the card through the reader. It spat out a receipt, but he ignored it. When she asked if he needed it, he just waved a hand dismissively and tucked his wallet back into his pocket before pushing the cart outside.

She took the receipt and looked it over, curious about him even though she had no evidence other than the fact that the man was rude to indicate he was in anyway involved in what happened to Marjorie.

The name at the top of it made her fingers tighten until the paper almost tore. That man was Benny Beckman, Marjorie's estranged stepson.

Valuable items had gone missing, and the man had just bought a lockbox. It could be a coincidence, but it could also be a clue.

Figuring out which it was wouldn't be easy, but she knew she had to try.

CHAPTER SIX

Flora wanted to ask Beth more about Benny Beckman, but it would have to wait. Today was Sydney's birthday, and she had offered to host. Violet was bringing the cake, and Grady was going to pick up some drinks on his way over after he left the hardware store that evening, which meant it was on her to get the food. It was the perfect fall day for a cookout, so she picked up bratwursts and ground beef from the butcher counter at the grocery store, along with some buns, salad, and some nice big russet potatoes for baking.

Once she got home, she focused on tidying up the house. She still needed to get nicer furniture, but she didn't know where to go for it. The estate sale probably would have been a bust even if Marjorie's death hadn't interrupted it -- the furniture there had been both too expensive and too fancy for what she needed. She might have to resort to buying a set of used furniture at an auction online and get it delivered. At least her current mismatched selection of furniture was fine for hosting her friends.

Once the house was tidy, she went outside and set up some camp chairs around the stone-lined fire pit in the grassy part of her backyard. Then she busied by herself by dragging dry wood from one of the debris piles in the tree line over, building up a pile of sticks and branches they could burn.

Getting ready for the bonfire made her realize she had forgotten to buy the ingredients for s'mores. Mentally kicking herself, she went back inside and sent a text message to Grady, asking if he could pick up marshmallows, chocolate bars, and graham crackers when he stopped at the store to get drinks.

She finished preparing for the party a couple of hours before her friends were due to start arriving and flopped down on the couch next to Amaretto, who had been watching haughtily from her favored seat at the top of the couch as she cleaned.

"I just realized," she said to the cat. "This will probably be one of our last fall bonfires. We won't be here next year. I don't know if the next house I buy will have a big enough yard to do something like this."

Amaretto rolled over onto her back, purring. Flora gingerly petted her belly, keeping an eye on the cat's claws in case it was a trick.

"I shouldn't get so sad whenever I think about selling the house," she continued. "This is what I wanted to do. It's *still* what I want to do. I loved working on the house, and I'm already eager to get started on the next one. I guess I've never really had a chance to make a place feel like my own before."

She had lived in apartments all of her adult life prior to this. Maybe she had put too much of herself into this house, which was what was making the thought of letting it go so difficult. Next time around, she would have to keep her eye on the game the whole time, and never forget that she was fixing the house to sell, not to live in.

She wished she could keep this house, and still have enough money to buy another fixer-upper to flip, but she *needed* the sale to afford the next house -- not to mention paying her aunt back.

Sighing, she kissed her cat's soft forehead and got up, heading upstairs to take a shower. She might be morose at the thought of selling this house, but she knew in her heart she was happier now than she had been before leaving Chicago and her mindless job there. She couldn't expect life to be perfect. It was already better than she had ever hoped it would be.

Her friends started arriving a little after seven. Flora, wearing her favorite pair of jeans and a maroon sweater, welcomed Violet and Sydney in. A pair of headlights down the road told her Grady wasn't far behind. Trusting him to let himself in -- and not let Amaretto escape while he was at it -- she joined Violet and Sydney in the kitchen, where Violet put a sheet cake in a box on the counter. While she checked it to make sure it hadn't been damaged in transport, Flora hugged Sydney.

"Happy Birthday! I hope you've had a good day so far."

"Thanks." He grinned. "It could be worse. I had to work, but it was an easy day, and I had this to look forward to. Thanks for hosting -- again. I feel like you always get stuck doing it."

"I enjoy it," she assured him. It was true -- she was proud of her house and property; she had worked hard on it, and didn't feel bad about how much she enjoyed showing it off. She also had the best home to host events like this, since the others all lived in apartments. Violet occasionally had everyone over for dinner, but they couldn't exactly have a bonfire in her living room.

The front door opened, announcing Grady's arrival, and she went to help him carry in the drinks.

"Hey, Grady," Violet said when they came back into the kitchen. "How are you doing?"

"Couldn't be better," he admitted as he put the drinks down on the counter while Flora made room in the fridge.

"Do you like the apartment?"

"Lovin' it. I can't complain about only having to cross the street to go to work, and I was getting mighty tired of living with my brother."

"How is Wade doing?"

"He's still trying to make money hauling scrap," Grady said, handing the drinks to Flora as she put them away. "He seems to be doing all right. I think he likes having the trailer to himself. He's working to get his record cleared. I think he's really turned over a new leaf this time."

"That's good," Violet said, smiling. "We're all pretty happy, aren't we? We should toast to how lucky we are -- but let's get the grill going first."

"I wasn't feeling very lucky last week," Flora said as she shut the fridge. "But you're right -- the four of us *are* pretty lucky, all things considered. I'll toast to that."

"Did you ever hear more about what happened to that woman?" Sydney asked as they went outside. The grill was under a cover next to the shed, but it didn't take long to remove the cover and ignite the propane burners. Flora fiddled with the dials, getting the flames going at a nice medium burn.

"Yes, actually," she said, giving Grady a meaningful look. She hadn't had a chance to tell him about the earlier call from Sherry. "I'll tell you about it while we get the burgers and brats ready."

By the time she was finished with her story -- including seeing Benny Beckman in the hardware store buying a lockbox -- the first burgers were sizzling on the grill.

"I remember looking at that painting," Grady said, frowning. "I don't remember if it was still there when we left, after calling the police."

"I don't either, and neither does Sherry," Flora said. "I mean, we were all distracted, so it makes sense. We weren't looking at art; we were all thinking about Marjorie. It does make me wonder if her death and the theft are tied together."

"Could be, or it could have been someone taking advantage of all the confusion," he said. "It's still possible she tripped and fell, and there was no foul play involved."

"I know," Flora said with a sigh. "I just feel like there's more and more that keeps coming to light, and all of it seems suspicious. Why was Benny there? Beth said Marjorie hated him, and the feeling was mutual."

"Well, his father's the one who died recently, right?" Violet chimed in. "Maybe he was there to pick up some of his things. He probably left *something* to his son in his will."

That was a good point, and not one Flora had thought of before. It might even explain why he had been so rude in pushing past Grady on the stairs -- she couldn't imagine how hard it would have been for him to have to pick up his estranged father's belongings from the woman who had broken up his parents' marriage and destroyed his relationship with the man.

"We can talk about it more later," Grady said. "This is a celebration, isn't it?"

"Right." Flora tried to get back into the right mood. "I'll pop inside and grab some plates. It looks like those burgers are almost done."

On her way back outside, the sound of a vehicle coming up the dirt road made her detour to peek around the side of her house. Traffic on her road this late at night was rare, and maybe the small town was getting to her, because she was always curious about who was driving by.

The sedan slowed as it reached her house, but then sped up again and passed it, only to pull into Beth's driveway a minute later. Flora squinted, but it was too far to see details. Whoever it was seemed to be a welcome guest, though, because she could just barely see the front door open and shut as Beth let them inside.

She wasn't sure she had ever seen Beth have guests so late before, and she hoped everything was all right. But Beth had her phone number, and Flora wasn't going to stoop to snooping on her neighbors, so she rejoined the others by the grill.

Grady was right. This was Sydney's birthday party. She could focus on other things any other day. Tonight was about her friends.

CHAPTER SEVEN

Flora had the morning to herself the next day; Grady had the early shift, and she didn't have to be at the hardware store until the afternoon. She slept in until Amaretto woke her up with plaintive meows, demanding breakfast.

Her friends had helped her clean up the evening before, but there were still a few dishes in the drying rack to put away, and the counter was lined with rinsed-out cans for her to recycle. She ignored all of that as she served Amaretto breakfast and made her coffee.

Only after she drained the last drops from her mug did she feel ready to start the day. She cleaned up the last of the mess in the kitchen, then went upstairs to shower and change into a pair of jeans and a t-shirt. She might not have to work this morning, but there *was* some stuff she wanted to get done. First on the list was visiting Beth. She wanted to ask more about Benny's relationship with his father and stepmother, and she was also curious about who had visited Beth so late last night. She wasn't quite sure how she felt about the second urge -- it was absolutely none of her business who her neighbor's guests were, but maybe Beth's love of gossip was rubbing off on her, because she desperately wanted to know.

First things first; breakfast. She ate a slice of leftover birthday cake, telling herself she would eat something more substantial before going to work. There were some cooked hamburger patties in her fridge and one last bratwurst, along with plenty of salad. Lunch could be her healthy meal. The birthday cake came from the new bakery in town, and it was *good*.

After her breakfast, she pulled on her shoes and slipped her cell phone into her back pocket, then stepped out the door. She decided to walk the distance to Beth's house; she was already feeling guilty about the breakfast of cake, and it wasn't as if she was in a hurry. It was a nice morning, anyway; the sky had huge, fluffy white clouds in it, there was a gentle breeze that carried the scent of autumn with it, and the air felt crisp and clean.

It only took a couple of minutes for her to reach Beth's house. She walked up the driveway, pausing to turn around and look at her property from this distant angle. It looked lovely, a white farmhouse standing in a neatly groomed lawn, the side and back of the yard lined with trees. She'd have to get a photo from this angle when she listed it; the house looked like it could have been on a magazine.

She turned back to Beth's house just in time to see a curtain twitch. A moment later, before she even reached the porch, the front door opened and Beth waved out at her.

"Good morning, Flora! Are you here to visit? I just put our breakfast away, but if you're hungry, I can heat up the leftovers for you."

"Oh, there's no need to do that," Flora said as she climbed the steps. Beth stepped back, inviting her inside, and she toed off her shoes after crossing the threshold. "I just thought I'd drop by for a chat, if you have time."

"Make yourself at home. Shall we sit in the kitchen? Do you want tea? Or maybe some warmed cider?"

"The cider sounds good," Flora said. She paused

by the living room to say hello to Tim, who was watching a sports show on the television, then followed Beth into the kitchen.

The older woman was already bustling around, preparing to heat up the apple cider in a saucepan. Flora took a step further into the kitchen, about to offer her help, when she froze.

There was a new painting hanging on the far wall of the kitchen. An all-too familiar painting, of a woman clothed in old Greek garb, lying in a field of flowers.

"No way," she whispered.

"What was that, dear?"

"Where did you get that?" She raised a shaking finger to point at the painting.

Beth turned her head to glance at it before refocusing on the cider, adding a sprinkle of cinnamon to it. "You sound just like Eloise. I found it. On the internet, just like you showed me."

She sounded proud of herself, and in other circumstances, Flora might have been impressed, but right now, all she could do was stare at the painting.

"It looks just like one Marjorie had," Beth continued as she stirred the cider. "I'm sure this one is just a copy, of course -- it was *much* too cheap to be an original -- but I think it goes quite nicely in here. Don't you?"

Flora shook her head, trying to snap herself out of her shock. "Beth, that painting was stolen from Marjorie's house!"

The older woman turned fully around to look at her, her expression disbelieving.

"What? No, that can't be right. Eloise visited just last night, and she didn't say anything about it. In fact, she mentioned seeing the painting at the estate sale, and congratulated me for finding such a nice reproduction of it."

"Trust me, the painting was stolen," Flora said. "The woman who was running the estate sale called me yesterday to tell me about it. The painting, some vases and figurines, and a set of nice silverware were all taken sometime the day Marjorie passed away."

Beth hesitated, her eyes darting from the painting and back to Flora. "Are you certain? No offense, dear, but Eloise was Marjorie's friend, and I'm quite certain she would have heard if something like that happened."

Flora opened her mouth, but then snapped it shut again, because Beth was right. Sherry had said she was calling everyone on her list, which would have included Eloise. The woman should have known about the missing items when she came here to visit Beth. So why hadn't she mentioned them?

"What was her visit about?" she asked, wondering if it had been something important enough to push the issues with Marjorie's death and the sale out of her mind.

"She just wanted to chat, and to tell me Marjorie's knitting club is holding a small memorial for her next weekend. I don't want to doubt you, Flora, but you must be mistaken. She was quite taken with the painting, and congratulated me for finding such a good deal and lovely reproduction. I certainly don't think she would have said that if it was *stolen*."

"I... maybe I'm thinking of the wrong painting?" she said, not really believing it. She was *certain* this was the same one, but Beth was equally certain it wasn't, and she was hard to argue with.

The older woman gave her a kind, almost pitying smile before turning back to the stove to stir the cider. "That's probably it, dear. If it makes you feel better, I'll ask Eloise about it the next time I see her."

"That would make me feel better," Flora admitted, taking a seat at the table. She slipped her phone out of her pocket, made sure the volume was turned down, then quickly took a picture of the painting before Beth turned back around. Just in case. "Did Eloise say anything about the argument she had with Marjorie the day of the estate sale?"

"No, she didn't mention a thing about that," Beth said. "She mentioned that Marjorie seemed content the last time she saw her, that's all."

Flora frowned. She was beginning to suspect that Eloise wasn't being all that truthful with Beth, but it was impossible to determine why. Was she trying to make Beth feel better about the passing of someone she had known for decades, or was she trying to hide something?

"One more question about the picture, then I'll drop it," she said as Beth carried over two mugs of cider. Flora accepted one gratefully. It smelled heavenly. "Who did you buy it from?"

Beth frowned. "His name was a jumble of words and letters online. He must have made a mistake when he was typing it in, so I'm not sure."

"Are you sure it was a man? Did you meet him?"

"I suppose it could have been a woman," Beth said. "I emailed them, whoever it was, and they were kind enough to drop the painting off for me. They told me to leave the cash in an envelope on the porch for them. I was a little uncertain about it all, but it worked out just fine."

Flora felt her eyelid twitch. Beth had given a

complete stranger, someone she had only emailed with, whose name she didn't even know, her address. Not only that, but she had also left an envelope of cash out for them. She was lucky she had gotten the painting at all. She was lucky she hadn't been *murdered.* Flora was going to need to give the older woman a crash course in internet safety.

"Can you forward me the emails they sent you?" she asked. If she had the person's email address, she could at least give it to the police and let them know about the painting. Maybe they could trace it back to the seller. "I'll show you how."

"I would, dear, but I always delete my emails when I'm done reading them. I don't want my computer's mailbox to get full."

Flora raised her cider to her lips slowly and took a sip, fighting the urge to let her forehead fall to the table in despair.

More computer lessons were definitely a priority, right after she figured out if this painting her neighbor was so proud of was actually stolen or not.

CHAPTER EIGHT

Yep, that's it.

The text from Sherry later that day confirmed what Flora already knew in her gut. Sitting in her truck in the hardware store's parking lot, she took a moment to reply before going inside.

I can go to the police with the photo, if you need me to. Beth was going to be upset when the police showed up to take the painting and her statement, but it needed to happen. Not only was the painting stolen, but the person who stole it might have had something to do with Marjorie's death.

Sherry's response came just a moment later. *No, I'll go to them later today. They have my original report already, so I should probably be the one who makes the follow-up report. What's your friend's name?*

Flora told her, then added, *She doesn't know it's stolen. Please make sure you're clear it's not her fault. She's a victim too. She got scammed.*

Sherry sent back a message assuring her she would, and Flora slipped her phone back into her pocket, grabbed her purse, and got out of the truck. She was stressed after her visit with Beth, and even more so because she realized she had forgotten to ask about Benny. Seeing the painting had completely thrown her off course.

When she stepped through the back entrance to the hardware store, she took a moment to ground herself. She was at work now. The problem of the painting was out of her hands; Sherry would deal with it, and Beth would just have to handle the revelation that it was stolen. Flora felt terrible for her -- she was sure the painting hadn't been cheap, even if the thief hadn't sold it for full price -- but what was done was done. She had done all she could.

Her mental pep talk made her feel a little better as she walked down the aisle to the front of the store. Grady was at the counter helping a customer check out, but gave her a warm smile in greeting. She smiled back, glad he was here. She would feel better after she told him everything.

He was just as taken aback by Beth's... interesting buying methods as she was.

"She's lucky something worse didn't happen," he grumbled. "I wonder if the seller still has listings online. Maybe the cops could find him that way."

"That's a good idea," she said. "*I* might be able to track them down that way."

He raised an eyebrow. "You'll be careful, right?"

"Don't worry. I'm *not* going to take a page out of Beth's book on this one. If I find any suspicious listings, I'll send them to Sherry or the police."

Ellison wasn't working that day, which meant she had the hardware store to herself after Grady left to go help his brother, Wade, with his scrap hauling business. It was an unusually busy day, so she didn't have much time to look online for the seller until later in the evening, when the rush died off an hour before close.

When she realized the hardware store was empty, she settled onto the stool behind the computer and loaded the web browser. Her elbow bumped the display of box cutters, and she moved it to the side, making a mental note to check on how many they had sold.

She went to the same website for local sales she had shown Beth and started scrolling through the list, not looking for anything in particular. The painting had been easy to recognize, but the other items were a little more vague. What she was hoping was to find a seller that was selling all the same items Sherry had told her were missing, even if they were in different listings.

She didn't get very far before the bell above the door jingled. She looked around to greet the newest customer, subtly clicking out of the web browser as she did so.

She was not expecting to see Eloise walk into the hardware store.

The older woman paused at the entrance to the store, looking around with a judgmental glint in her eyes before turning her attention on Flora.

"Are you Flora Abner?" she asked, coming up to the counter. "Beth York's neighbor?"

"That's me," Flora said. "How can I help you?"

"Beth called me earlier today and related all sorts of nasty rumors you've been spreading about me," Eloise said, crossing her arms. "I want to know why. I've never done nothing to hurt you. I didn't even know your name before today."

Flora gaped at her, feeling a pang at the thought of

Beth calling this woman to complain about her. Of course, that probably wasn't how it happened – Beth was probably confused and concerned when Flora left that morning, and had called her friend to get to the truth of things.

It was Flora's fault for not thinking that might happen. If someone implied one of her friends was lying or hiding something, of course she would call them to get to the truth of the matter.

"I promise, I haven't been telling any lies about you," Flora said. "I don't have anything against you. I was just trying to help Beth."

"Well now she's thinking of going to the police to see if her lovely painting was stolen," Eloise said. "And she asked if I argued with Marjorie right before her death. I don't even know where you got that from. You say you're not telling any fibs, but you certainly seem to be making things up."

"I was at the estate sale," Flora explained. "I heard you arguing with Marjorie. You slammed a door right before you came down the stairs, and you walked right past me and my boyfriend."

Eloise pressed her lips together. "Well, whether you were there or not, you still don't know what you're talking about. Maybe it sounded like an argument to you, but I assure you, that's how Marjorie and

I spoke to each other. We didn't need to use false niceties to say what we wanted to say. We were straight with each other. If I thought she was making a mistake, then I told it like I saw it. And I don't regret that, even if it did end up being our last conversation."

"What mistake did you think she was making?" Flora asked, curious.

The older woman sniffed. "That is none of your business. I know you're new to Warbler, but you need to learn to keep your nose out of things you aren't involved in. Now you've got Beth all worried, and for all I know, you've been going around saying the same thing to other people. I just lost a dear friend. I don't need you going around implying that I'm lying about something, or that I might have had something to do with her death."

Flora winced at her words, and the motion made the older woman's eyes narrow.

"*Have* you been going around saying that?" she asked slowly. "You eavesdropped on what you thought was an argument, then you go slinking around telling people I argued with my friend, and I must have murdered her too. I really don't know what Beth sees in you. You're just a horrible, nosy gossip like all the other young folk in town."

"I haven't been gossiping about any of this," Flora snapped, finally losing her temper. "I saw the painting when I went over to Beth's house, and of course I was worried, because I recognized it and I knew it had been stolen. I still don't know why you didn't say anything about that. And you have to admit, if you look at it from my perspective, it does seem a little suspicious that you got into a shouting match with your so-called friend, and Grady and I found her passed away just a few minutes later. I don't have anything against you, I'm just trying to figure out what's going on."

"How on earth was I supposed to know the painting was stolen?" Eloise snapped. "It's not as if the newspaper released a story on it. You have no idea what you're talking about. If anyone had something to do with Marjorie's passing, it was that woman who was running the estate sale for her. She was terrible at her job, and Marjorie let her know it. I watched her get more and more upset all morning. By the time I left, she was positively seething. If you're going to go sticking your nose into stuff you have no business investigating, I suggest that you start bothering her and leave me alone."

With that, she turned on her heel and yanked the hardware store's front door open, making the bells jingle wildly as she stepped outside and stalked away down the sidewalk.

Flora stared after her, feeling equal parts chagrined and intrigued.

She assumed Eloise knew about the theft from Marjorie's house, since Sherry had told her she was calling all of the numbers on her list. If Eloise really didn't know, that meant Sherry had lied to her.

She was almost certain that *one* of them was lying, and she wanted to figure out which it was.

CHAPTER NINE

A chat with Sherry was going to be her best bet for getting to the bottom of things. She sent her a text message, asking if she would be able to meet after work. The other woman's response came sometime between Flora logging out of the computer and locking the doors.

I'm just leaving the office, and I'm going to grab dinner. If you want to meet with me, I'll be at the new cheesesteak restaurant in 15 minutes.

Perfect, I'll see you there, Flora texted back before grabbing her store keys and making sure everything was locked up.

She needed to know what was going on. This wasn't just plain curiosity anymore – if one of Beth's friends was involved in what happened to Marjorie, then Beth could be in danger, especially since she had acquired the missing painting. She couldn't understand why Eloise would have lied when she said she hadn't heard about the theft, but she also couldn't see why Sherry would have lied about calling everyone on the list. There might be something she was missing, and she wasn't going to rest easy until she knew what it was.

The cheesesteak restaurant was in the same spot where her old, favorite sandwich shop had been. She didn't know what Sherry's car looked like, so she went in when she got there. Sherry wasn't there yet, but Flora put in a to go order and got a table anyway. It would save her heating up leftovers for dinner, at least. As much as she liked hamburgers and bratwurst, she'd had some of the leftovers for lunch, and wasn't in the mood for the same thing tonight.

Sherry arrived a few minutes later, looking stressed and harried as she glanced around the room. She spotted Flora, waved, and went to the counter to put in her order. After paying, she sat across the table from Flora.

"Sorry, I'm in a bit of a rush," she said. "What did you want to talk about? Did you find more of the missing items?"

"No," Flora said. "I *am* looking, though. I was

hoping you could answer some questions for me about someone I ran into while I was at the estate sale. Two people, actually. The first is Benny Beckman. He's —"

"Marjorie's stepson," Sherry said with a sigh. "I know. What about him?"

"Well, did he say anything to you when he signed in?"

"He didn't sign in," Sherry said. "Family doesn't have to. He probably wouldn't have signed in even if I had tried to make him, though. He... well, I'll just say he wasn't in the best of moods."

"Do you know why? I'm aware that Marjorie didn't get along with him, and it made me wonder what he even wanted there."

Sherry looked down at the table and seemed to come to a decision. "I'm probably going to be losing my job anyway, so I guess this doesn't matter. He had a paper he said was from his father's will, naming him as the inheritor of half of the estate. He said he needed to talk to his stepmother, and that I should be prepared to halt the sale. It was just a printed-out piece of paper, though; I got the feeling it wasn't legitimate."

She remembered the paper, and the information answered some of her questions. The timeline was alarming, though. Benny had arrived, already upset, to try to stop the estate sale, and then Marjorie was found dead by herself and Grady just minutes after he charged up the stairs… maybe she was wrong about Eloise being involved.

"Hold on, why did you say you're probably going to lose your job?" she asked, suddenly realizing what the other woman had said.

"The estate sale company I work for has financial problems," she said, her tone defeated. "This was supposed to be a big moneymaker for us. We get a percentage of the proceeds from the sale. In a town like Warbler, there usually aren't a lot of high-ticket items at sales like these, but Marjorie and her husband were well off. We were on the verge of closing our doors when Marjorie called us. But then the sale fell through, and now we're looking at missing items, and we're being forced to cancel the items people put deposits on. It's a huge mess. I'm probably going to be out of a job by this time next month."

"I'm sorry," Flora said. "That's horrible. I can't even imagine."

"I wish I had never agreed to run the sale for her," Sherry said vehemently. "It was horrible from start to finish. She's one of the worst people I've ever had to work with, I should have shut the whole thing down when her son arrived with that paper. I was really hoping we would be able to recover all of the stolen items, but if we can't, the company is going to be contractually obligated to pay the sum of the loss to the estate."

"Hopefully the fact that the painting has been found helps," Flora said.

The other woman sighed again. "I haven't even had time to go to the police about that yet. I'll have to do it tomorrow. Of course, if the woman who bought it fights the seizure, it's going to be even more of an expense. We'll have to get experts in to determine if it's not a replica or reproduction, and even after the police are finally able to seize it, they will probably hold it in evidence for who knows how long before returning it to the estate. I'm sorry for venting. This has been the worst week of my life."

"It's all right," Flora said. "Thank you for telling me all of this."

"Why are you so interested? I didn't know you knew her."

"Like I said before, I'm friends with the woman who bought the painting. I'm worried about her, and I don't want her to get involved in something messy like this."

Sherry gave a bitter laugh. "It's a bit too late for that now."

A server came up with their food, both orders in to-go bags – it seemed Sherry was planning on eating hers at home as well. Before the other woman could get up, Flora said, "There's something else I want to ask you."

"Go on. I'm going to turn my phone off once I get home and try to forget about all of this for a while, so this is your only chance."

"I spoke to someone else who was at the estate sale that morning, and they had no idea about the missing items. Didn't you say were going to call everyone on the list?"

"Only people who signed in during the last half-hour before it ended," Sherry explained. "It wouldn't make any sense to call someone who arrived when we opened at eight and left before a single item went missing."

"I see. Thanks again, Sherry. I hope things start looking up for you."

"Me too," Sherry said as she grabbed her bag. Flora watched her leave, then carried her own bag out to the parking lot.

It seemed neither Sherry nor Eloise was lying. That was probably a good thing, but it also meant she had no idea who might be responsible for the thefts and possibly even Marjorie's death. She was still unsure about Benny. The circumstances of his arrival, and the timing of it, still seemed suspicious, but she couldn't understand why he would steal a few items to sell a few days later. If he was supposed to inherit half of the estate, then wasn't that just like stealing from himself?

She didn't envy Sherry for having to deal with all of this. It was a huge mess, and she was glad that the most drama she had to deal with on a daily basis was Grady ordering way too many box cutters.

She would stick with house flipping and running the hardware store, and made a mental note to stay far away from the estate sale business.

CHAPTER TEN

While she was still in the parking lot, she called Grady and asked if he wanted her to pick up a cheesesteak for him as well, but he was in the next town over with his brother, trying to load the remains of a mangled lawnmower into the bed of his truck. He was essentially working two jobs while he tried to help his brother get his business on its feet, which meant she hadn't been able to see him as much as she would have liked, but she could hardly begrudge him that. She technically had two jobs too, even if the work on her house was all but done now. As soon as she started on the next house, she would be a lot busier.

She went home and tried not to feel lonely as she ate her cheesesteak on the couch in front of the TV while Amaretto stared at her from the coffee table. She still needed to find some good furniture, but it wasn't urgent, since she wasn't going to list the house until spring.

"Well, that was a good sandwich, but I feel kind of gross after eating all of it," she said once she was done, dabbing at her lips with a napkin. Amaretto sniffed the cheesesteak wrapper and jumped off the table disdainfully.

"Where are you going? Let's take a walk. We'll go *outside*."

The cat flicked her tail and walked over to the front door, recognizing the words. Flora felt a surge of affection for her. Amaretto might not be as obedient as a dog, but she was smart in her own way. After all, how many cats learned to walk on a harness?

After strapping said harness onto her cat, the two of them left through the front door and looped around to the back of the house, setting out on the forest path Flora had painstakingly carved through the woods with a brush eater. It had been an exhausting project, but the results were worth it. She now had a lovely nature trail of her very own, leading back to the pond at the rear of the property. She hoped whoever bought the house after her enjoyed it as much as she did.

They lingered around the pond when they reached

it, Amaretto cautiously sniffing the water while being careful not to get her feet wet. Flora gazed at the newly cleaned pond, her heart full with pride and happiness. Sure, she hadn't dredged the pond with her own two hands, mostly because she physically couldn't have done it by herself, but after clearing the path to it, she had hired a company to come out and do it for her.

The pond, which had once been overgrown, full of green sludge and fallen tree limbs, and more trash than she wanted to think about, was now clean enough to swim in. She would have to treat the water for algae and mosquitoes next year, but even now it was a far cry from the mess it had once been. The base to the gazebo she and Grady were planning on working on over the winter had already been set down, and they had marked out the edge of what would become of the beach. She was still price shopping for a good deal on a delivery of sand, since squelching through the mud that currently ringed the pond wasn't much fun for anyone.

The entire project should be done just before she sold the house, which unfortunately meant she probably wouldn't be able to enjoy it very much.

Once Amaretto lost interest in the scents and sights of nature, they walked back to the house and

Flora grabbed her laptop before settling down in front of the television again. She wanted to get back to scouring the local sales page. She wasn't sure how much help it would be, but at least it was something she could do.

She found what she was looking for almost exactly half an hour later. The sun had begun to go down, and she had just sat back down from turning on the lamp when she spotted it. A listing for the sale of a silverware set – *real silver*, the ad read. She clicked the seller's name and felt her heart rate increase when she saw what else they were selling. Two expensive looking vases and a collection of figurines. This had to be it. This had to be the person Beth had bought the painting from. Their username even matched her description – a seemingly random string of numbers and letters.

She wished she had thought to ask Beth to write down what she remembered of the person's username, but that was an easy problem to solve. Gently removing Amaretto from her lap, she tucked her laptop under her arm, grabbed her keys and her phone, and went outside to get into her truck. No walking this time; she was too excited to spend the time it would take. She drove the short distance between their houses and parked in Beth's driveway.

Her neighbor's lights were still on, and Beth dropped by on her unannounced all the time, so she had no qualms about walking right up to the front door and knocking.

It took a couple of minutes for Beth to answer. She seemed surprised but pleased to see Flora and invited her in.

"Twice in one day," she said. "I'm so happy you're coming out of your shell, dear."

Flora didn't think she had been particularly withdrawn before, but she supposed there was something to be said about the difference between Southern hospitality and what passed for it back in Chicago.

"I think I found the person you bought the painting from," she said as she slipped her shoes off. "Can you look at their username and tell me if you recognize it?"

"This again?" Beth's face fell slightly. "I suppose. I don't know why you're getting involved with all of this, though."

"It's just something I need to do," Flora said. She joined Beth at the kitchen table and opened her laptop, logging in before turning the screen to face the other woman. "Here. Is this the person you bought it from?"

The older woman squinted at the laptop screen.

"Yes, I think that was their name. I wonder what they were trying to type. It seems like they're about as good at using the keyboard as I am." She chuckled.

"They were probably trying to stay anonymous," Flora explained. "You're sure this is them?"

"I'm very sure, dear. Who wouldn't remember a name like that?"

"Would you be willing to go to the police station with me in the morning?" she asked.

Sherry had *said* she was going to go in, but the woman had all day and hadn't done it yet. She didn't know if the woman was stalling for some reason, or if she was just too overwhelmed to do what needed to be done.

"I still don't think you're right about the painting being stolen," Beth said. "But I'll humor you. If you pick me up, I'll go into town with you tomorrow."

"Thank you," Flora said as she shut the laptop. "Really, Beth. I know you don't think I'm right about this, but I'm onto something. I can feel it. Oh, before I go, I talked to Eloise today. She came into the hardware store, and was pretty upset."

Beth frowned. "Did she? I'm sorry, dear. I didn't mean to make her upset with you. I just wanted to ask her about some of the things you said, and I didn't see anything wrong with giving her your name when she asked who had been talking about her. I hope she wasn't too unpleasant."

Flora winced. "Well, she didn't stay for very long, at least. In the future, please don't give people my name or my address, or tell them where I work without talking to me first, all right?"

"I'll try to remember," Beth said. "What if they have a delivery for you, though? What if it's something urgent?"

"Then you can call me," Flora said firmly. "Please, it's important to me."

"All right, dear. I'll keep that in mind."

Flora didn't find that quite as reassuring as she would have liked, but she suspected it was the best she was going to get. She thanked Beth again, promised to come over at ten o'clock sharp, and let herself out of the house.

She was so close to figuring out the truth of what had happened to Marjorie and the missing items, she could almost taste it.

CHAPTER ELEVEN

Flora was woken by a ringing phone just after seven-thirty the next morning. It was always stressful to be woken up by an unexpected call, but at the sight of Beth's number on her phone screen, her worries abated somewhat. She probably just wanted to make sure Flora was up – she seemed to have the idea that Flora would sleep until noon if she didn't set an alarm.

"Hello?" she said as she answered the call, trying not to sound as if she had just woken up.

"Oh good, you're awake," the older woman said. "Would you be terribly put out if I asked you to drive me into town early? I need to pick something up before we go to the police station."

"Yeah, I can do that," Flora said, rubbing the sleep out of her eyes. "How soon do you want to leave?"

"I'm ready whenever you can get over here."

"I'll be there in about half an hour," she replied. "Is that good enough?"

The older woman made a displeased noise. "Well, if that's the best you can do."

"It is," Flora said firmly. As it was, she would be rushing to shower, get ready for the day, drink her coffee, and feed her cat before getting out the door. She said a quick goodbye to Beth and hopped out of bed, detouring to the kitchen to feed Amaretto and turn the coffee maker on before going back upstairs to take her shower.

Before leaving the house, she poured her coffee into a thermos and sipped it as she walked out to her truck. She no longer felt half-asleep, which was nice, but she still didn't appreciate being woken up before her alarm even went off. She didn't think it was that odd to sleep in when she didn't have any early commitments, but Beth was up every day before the sun rose. Despite her friendship with the older woman, there were some things they would never see eye to eye on.

Beth was waiting on her porch when Flora pulled into the driveway, and was already walking toward the truck before Flora even put it into park. She hopped into the passenger seat and settled her purse on her lap before buckling up.

"Where are we going?" Flora asked.

"I'll direct you," Beth assured her. "Just head toward town for now."

Beth was acting weird, but Flora wasn't in the mood to pry. She pulled out of the driveway and headed down the road to Warbler. As they neared the main intersection, Beth said, "Turn right, then turn left on the second street. You're looking for Warbler Community Park."

"I know where that is."

She made the turn and headed toward the park, slowing as she neared it, not sure if Beth wanted her to go there, or if their destination was just near it.

"You should park across the street, but make sure you're facing the park," Beth said.

Flora did as Beth requested and left her truck running once they were parked. "All right, what is this about? I thought you needed to get some groceries or pick up a prescription or something. Why are we at a park at eight in the morning?"

"You'll see," Beth said with far too much eagerness in her voice as she gazed out the windshield. The park was mostly empty this early; there was one person jogging and someone else walking their dogs, but that was it.

"Beth," Flora said slowly. "I'm not kidding. What are we doing here?"

Beth glanced over at her and seemed to realize Flora was going to require an answer to her question.

"I decided to figure this out for myself, once and for all," Beth said. "You made me start to wonder about that painting. If it *was* stolen, then whoever stole it needs to face the consequences for their actions. I thought we could see who shows up with the silverware today."

"The what?" Flora asked, even more confused.

"I sent an email to that person with the odd name," Beth explained. "I told them I was interested in buying that lovely set of silverware they had. I didn't want them coming back to my house, considering that they might be a criminal and all, so they agreed to drop it off for me in the park. They were even kind enough to walk me through sending them the money through the internet."

"Okay, first, you should never do that," Flora said. "How did you send the money? No, you should just go talk to your bank after this. I don't want them to drain your account. And second, is this some sort of sting?"

"They're supposed to have the box sitting on that bench right there by nine," Beth said, pointing at said bench. "They won't realize we're here early, and that we're watching."

This was so incredibly shady, Flora had no idea how the person had managed to convince Beth to go through something similar with the painting. Still, despite everything, she was a little impressed that the older woman had set this up.

"And we're just going to watch, right?" Flora asked. "I don't want you jumping out of the truck when they show up."

"That's right," Beth said. "You can use that fancy phone of yours to take a photo when they get here. I'll take the box of silverware right to the police station. Maybe they'll be able to dust it for fingerprints."

It was a terrible plan, and Flora wished Beth had let her know what was going on before they set off from her house. Sighing, she leaned back in her seat and let her gaze wander across the park. If they could get a picture of whoever dropped off the silverware – assuming they didn't just take Beth's money and run – it would probably be an open and closed case. That might help Sherry, at least, if the company she worked for didn't have to pay for the loss of the items.

Maybe it was the thought of Sherry that made her notice it, but as her eyes wandered over the street, she spotted a tiny storefront with a sign hanging over the entrance that read *Lorelei's Estate Solutions*. She realized that must be the estate sale company where Sherry worked – she couldn't imagine there being two of them in Warbler.

Was it a coincidence that it was right across the street from the park where the silverware drop-off was happening? But why would *Sherry* steal the items? It seemed like it was causing far more trouble than it was worth, considering she might lose her job over it.

Flora frowned. It had actually sounded like Sherry was on the verge of losing her job anyway. Had she stolen those items with the intent to sell them for the cash she might need when the estate sale company closed?

Or maybe she hadn't planned it at all. Maybe she had gotten into an argument with Marjorie and something had happened – a shove, or maybe Marjorie had simply stepped wrong and fallen, hitting her head on the way down. Sherry might have panicked and, realizing that this would almost certainly mean the loss of her job, she might have helped herself to a few expensive looking things on the way out.

A thrill of excitement rushed through Flora. It all made sense. She was *certain* she had it, but the next few minutes would tell them for sure.

She was so lost in her thoughts that she almost missed it when someone in a light blue minivan pulled into the park's parking lot. It was only when Beth shifted in her seat, looking forward eagerly, that she noticed it, and immediately recognized the van that had peeled away from Marjorie's house as Flora was helping shut down the estate sale.

This van's presence told her it almost *had* to have something to do with the theft. But Sherry had still been in the house when the van left. She couldn't have been the one driving it. Did that mean she was working with someone else, or was Flora wrong about her?

Someone got out of the van and walked around to the back, popping the hatch to take something out. Tucking the cardboard box under their arm and leaving the hatch open, the hooded figure started walking down the path toward the park bench.

With their hood pulled over their head, she couldn't figure out who it was. To make matters worse, the van was parked at such an angle that she couldn't see the license plate.

"Stay here," Flora said as she unbuckled her seatbelt.

"Where are you going?" Beth asked.

"I'm going to walk past the van and take a look at the license plate. Then I'm going to pretend that I'm here to jog around the park. Hopefully whoever that is won't think anything of it. You keep an eye out, and if anything happens, call the police." She pressed the cell phone into Beth's hands and got out of her truck, doing her best to look casual as she crossed the street.

She couldn't take a picture of the license plate, since she left her phone with Beth, but she was certain she could memorize it. She stepped up the curb, crossed the patch of grass, and stepped back down into the parking lot, glancing over toward the bench. The person the hood was just bending over to put the box on it. She was a little amazed at their honesty – twice now, they could have easily taken money from Beth and not given her the items she was buying, but both times they had actually delivered. Maybe they didn't want the added scrutiny from the police if they scammed someone out of an item.

Finally, she reached the van. She paused, bending down to pretend to tie her shoe, and looked up at the license plate. She mentally repeated the digits, then gazed into the open trunk.

There were a few vases, more than had been listed online, and an open box with a jumble of figurines in it. And something else.

A lockbox. A lockbox she recognized, because she had sold it to Benny Beckman only a couple of days ago.

CHAPTER TWELVE

The lockbox. Even though it was possible someone else out there had the same model – the hardware store sold them, after all, and they could hardly be the only place that did – she knew in her gut it had to belong to Benny.

Which meant the van belonged to Benny. He was the one who was currently dropping off the box of silverware on the park bench.

She straightened up, turning to walk back toward the truck before remembering that she had been planning on going for a quick jog, in order to pretend to be just another visitor to the park. She paused, turning awkwardly around again, but before she could get far, someone called out her name.

"Flora!"

She was so wound up that she jumped as she twisted to see Sherry waving at her from the sidewalk in front of the estate sale company. The woman looked both ways down the street, then crossed it, walking toward Flora. She couldn't just walk away now – Sherry was sure to call out to her again – so she would have to hope Benny didn't recognize her. She met Sherry at the edge of the parking lot.

"I thought I recognized you," the woman said. "I'm just getting to work. What are you doing out here?"

"I…" There was no way she could tell the truth; even though she was relatively sure Sherry didn't have anything to do with the theft now, the whole thing would just take too much explanation. "I was just thinking of going for a jog."

"In your jeans?" She looked down Flora's pants. "Oh, well, I suppose it's a nice morning for it. Listen, I wanted to tell you I'm going to head to the police station as soon as I talk to my boss. If you know anything else –"

She broke off, her gaze going over Flora's shoulder. Flora turned to see Benny, still with his hood pulled up, though his face was recognizable from this distance, returning to his van. He paused when he saw them. He might not have recognized her on her own, but he definitely seemed to recognize Sherry.

"What's going on?" Sherry asked, her brows drawing together as she looked between the two of them. "You're not here for a jog, are you? You were meeting him here."

"No," Flora said quickly. "I had no idea he was going to be here."

That was true, at least; she hadn't expected to find Benny, *specifically*, here.

Benny quickly shut the back of the van, but it was too late; Sherry must have seen what was inside of it. Her eyes were wide and she took a step back.

"You're working together. The two of you stole that stuff. All this time, I've been confiding in you, I thought you were helping me – you've been involved all along."

"No, Sherry, I swear –" Flora broke off as Sherry took another step back and rummaged in her purse, pulling out a cell phone. She tapped on the screen and shakily entered her passcode.

"I'm calling the police. I can't believe this. How could you sit across from me and act like you understood, when you've been behind this all along?"

"What are you doing?" Benny asked, jogging over to them. "Hey, lady, stop that."

He moved to grab the phone out of Sherry's hand, but she jerked back. Flora shot a glance toward her truck, but she couldn't see what Beth was doing. She sorely regretted leaving her cell phone with the other woman.

"Don't touch me," Sherry snapped. "I can't believe it. I should've known –"

Benny lunged forward again, this time managing to tear her phone out of her hands. He threw it to the ground, and the screen shattered. That was enough to break her out of her shock, and she backed away from him. He looked between her and Sherry, his eyes wide and panicked.

"How did you find me? One of you sent that email, didn't you? I should've been more careful."

"I don't understand," Sherry said. "Why would you do this? Did one of you *kill* her? She might not have been a very kind person, but she didn't deserve to *die*."

"Sherry, I'm not working with him!" Flora exclaimed. "I was trying to figure out who the thief was. I'm the one who arranged to meet him here, and I got here early to see who dropped off the silverware he was selling."

That wasn't exactly true, since Beth had set all

this up, but she wasn't going to throw the older woman under the bus. Even if this was all her fault.

Sherry hesitated, but Benny didn't. He stooped down to grab the broken cell phone and shoved it into his pocket before taking a step away from them, his hands clenched into fists.

"Neither of you are going to say anything," he said, his tone dark. "If either of you go to the police, I'll... I'll hunt you down. I'm not losing everything, not again."

"Of course we're going to the police," Sherry screeched. "You stole thousands of dollars' worth of goods!"

Benny tensed; that obviously wasn't what he had wanted to hear. Flora raised her hands in a calming gesture. "Maybe we can figure this out," she said. "Maybe you could give everything back?"

He scoffed. "Are you stupid? I need the money. That hag stole *everything* from me. She took my family, she took my inheritance, and she didn't even care that my father had meant to leave me half of everything. She paid for it in the end, but that wasn't enough. Do you have any idea what it's like living paycheck to paycheck while I have to drive past the huge house she shared with my father every day?"

"What do you mean, she paid for it?" Flora asked.

"Did you kill her?" She had suspected Marjorie's death wasn't the accident it seemed, but there had never been any proof.

"You have no idea how long I've wanted to hit her ugly face," he spat. "I had my father's *will* with me. He didn't have time to get it certified by a lawyer, but it's what he wanted. She should have respected his last wishes."

Sherry pressed her hands to her lips, moaning in fear as she realized Benny was a murderer, not just a thief.

This was not going well. "You didn't mean to kill her," Flora said, trying to calm things down. "Just tell the police what happened, maybe you can take a plea deal –"

"No!" He slammed his fist into his thigh. "I'm done always getting the short end of the stick. I'm forty years old! I've got nothing to show for it. I don't have any more money now than I did when I was twenty. I drive a *minivan*. I spent the last few years working on my relationship with my father, but he died just before he could give his lawyer the updated will. That hag he called his wife took *everything* from me. I don't regret what I did to her. I should have done it a long time ago."

"You killed her and then you stole what you could

carry," Sherry whispered. "Why? I know the prices of those items. It's a few thousand dollars, but it's not going to make you rich."

"It would've been enough for me to get out of here, move out of state, and start somewhere new," he said. "I can't stay here any longer."

"You had to realize someone would put it together eventually," Flora said quietly.

"I was going to disappear. Take all the money in my account out in cash, throw all my important belongings in the van, and just leave." That must have been what the lockbox was for – if he was taking all his money out of the bank, he would have wanted somewhere safe to keep it. "And now I'm losing everything again, it's all because of the two of you."

He took a step toward them and Sherry backpedaled. Flora took a step back as well, not sure what he intended. He didn't have a weapon, which she was grateful for, but he could still overpower them.

A very familiar "Yoo-hoo," sounded behind them, and she craned her neck to see Beth walking across the street, Flora's cell phone held up in her hand.

"It looks like I'm interrupting something," she called as she crossed the street. "But I wanted to let you know the police are on their way. I called them and told them a man is threatening two women in a parking lot."

Benny cursed under his breath, and turned to rush back to his van. This time, Flora made a point of making sure she had the license plate memorized. Then he kicked the van into reverse and she quickly grabbed Sherry's arm, pulling her onto the grass so they could duck behind a tree if he tried to take his anger out on them.

Thankfully, he was more concerned with escaping. The van's tires squealed as he pulled away down the road, leaving Beth standing on the grassy curb, gazing after him. Flora's heart was pounding as she walked across the parking lot to the older woman.

"Thank goodness for you, Beth," she said. "How soon will they be here?"

Beth tittered. "Oh, I didn't actually call them. I couldn't figure out how to work your phone. I thought pretending I did would work well enough."

Despite everything, Flora took her phone back with a laugh. "Thanks, Beth. You really saved our skins."

Flora stood in the center of her living room, her hands on her hips. The new furniture, which Grady had spotted at a yard sale while he was out hauling scrap with Wade, fit the living room well. It was a matching set, with pale wood and cream-colored cushions, and it looked a lot nicer than her old set, which was now safely stored in the shed.

It felt good to have it, even if it was another reminder that the house wouldn't be hers for much longer.

"Thanks again," she said to Grady. "I don't want to think about how much it would have cost me if I had to buy this at an online auction."

"You can thank Wade for spotting it," Grady said, dropping an arm around her shoulders and pulling her close. "I'm surprised he remembered it – I think I mentioned you were looking for new furniture once. He's not a bad guy, not really."

"I'll have to invite him over for dinner the next time we have people over," she said. Her lips pulled down in a frown. "Though I am still bummed I missed out on that rug. It really would've been perfect in the hall."

"There's no chance you could go back and buy it?"

She shook her head. "I have no idea what's happening with everything Marjorie owned, but from what Sherry said, it's a mess. Inheritance law sounds complicated. I think if she had died of natural causes, Benny might have had a chance to inherit some of it, since she was married to his father, but apparently killing her makes him ineligible for that."

"I'm glad they caught him before he got too far. I guess if you push anyone far enough, they'll break eventually."

She sighed, leaning her head back against his shoulder. "I can understand why he hated her so much – she didn't sound like a pleasant person. But I can't see myself ever making the same choices he did. It's one thing to hate someone; it's another to actually hurt them. And not just Marjorie – I know it's not the same, but he hurt everyone he sold the stolen items to as well."

"How's Beth handling the loss of her painting?"

"She's not up as upset as I thought she would be," Flora admitted. "I think she likes having a new story to tell to her friends."

He chuckled. "Somehow, that doesn't surprise me. I'm glad she's a fast thinker. It sounds like you were in a pretty bad situation, and she stepped up."

"Yeah. That's what I get for thinking something couldn't possibly go wrong. You know, come to think of it, she's the one who got me into this whole mess in the first place. I only went to Marjorie's estate sale at her suggestion."

"Sounds like she's a bad influence on you."

She giggled, pulling away so she could rearrange one of the couch cushions. "Well, I've learned my lesson. The next time she has an idea, I don't think I'll be quite so quick to agree to it."